THE EYE OF YORK
In medieval times this was the centre of the castle courtyard or bailey. Later, parliamentary elections were held here and the successful candidates' names declared (pages 22–23)

THE FEMALE PRISON (1780)
Designed by the York architect John Carr, the building today houses part of York Castle Museum (page 22)

THE DEBTORS' PRISON (1705)
Designed by William Wakefield, the prison originally housed both debtors and felons; the yard at the back was used for executions after 1868 (page 22)

CONTENTS

SOUTH GATE
This twin-towered gateway gave access to the rivers Ouse and Foss, the King's Mill, St George's chapel and the Fishergate suburb (page 9)

THE CASTLE WALLS
Two corner towers of the curtain wall survive together with the foundations of the main south gate (page 9)

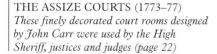

THE ASSIZE COURTS (1773–77)
These finely decorated court rooms designed by John Carr were used by the High Sheriff, justices and judges (page 22)

TOP *Clifford's Tower on its mound, with part of the Assize Courts on the left*

1

INTRODUCTION

YORK HAD BEEN THE CENTRE of a Viking kingdom during the tenth century, and even under Anglo-Saxon rule in the eleventh century it continued to attract Viking claimants and adventurers. In September 1066 the latest of these claimants arrived in the form of Harald Hardrada, son of a Norwegian king. He was fought off by the English king, Harold Godwineson, who defeated the invaders at Stamford Bridge, east of York. The following month, however, Harold in his turn was defeated by the Normans at Hastings.

William the Conqueror's victory did not automatically bring the rest of the country under his control, and the Normans still had to subdue the Saxons and Vikings in the northern counties. The new king came to York in 1068, building a castle there and granting land to his leading Norman barons. After a serious revolt in 1069 William came north again, repairing his first castle and erecting a second one, so that between them the castles could control the passage up the river Ouse from the sea.

The two castles were of motte-and-bailey design. The motte was an artificial earth mound which supported a tall wooden look-out tower. The bailey was a spacious courtyard which contained all the timber buildings necessary to sleep and provision the garrison. Both castles were surrounded by ditches; at the main fortress these were filled with water from the nearby river, while at the secondary castle they were dry.

The castle to which Clifford's Tower belongs is likely to have been the earlier

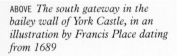

ABOVE *The south gateway in the bailey wall of York Castle, in an illustration by Francis Place dating from 1689*

RIGHT *York as it may have appeared in the fifteenth century. This reconstruction drawing by E Ridsdale Tate, drawn in 1914, clearly shows the two castles guarding the passage up the river Ouse. Clifford's Tower and its bailey (to the right) are built in stone and strongly defended by outer ditches and walls, but Baile Hill (to the left) has deteriorated to little more than an earth mound. Note the protective walls around the outer perimeter of the city*

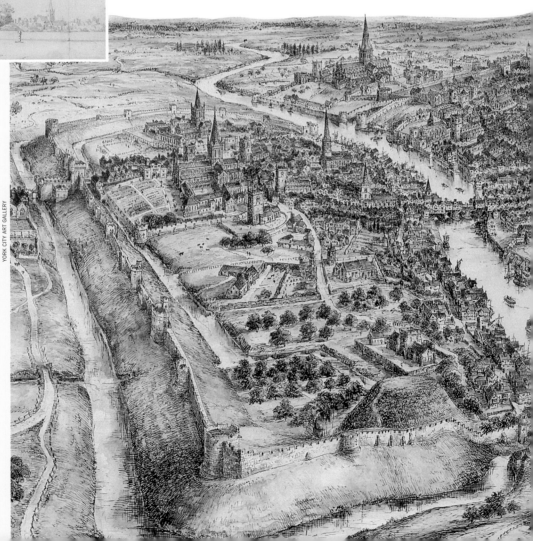

LEFT *The interior of Clifford's Tower today*

BELOW *The interior of the tower as it may have appeared when first completed in the late thirteenth century (drawing: Peter Dunn, after a drawing by Peter Snowball)*

Doorway to the **chapel**

The **upper floor** housed the king's private apartments

The **entrance** was in this tower

Three **latrines** or toilets emptied outside the tower

A wooden **palisade** protected the base of the tower

The **ground floor** contained the guard-room and offices for royal clerks

ABOVE *Looking north towards the Minster, with the spire of St Mary Castlegate in the foreground*

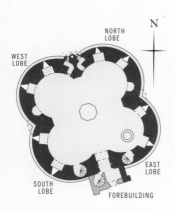

Upper Floor

The upper floor contained the king's private rooms when he was in residence, and housed the royal clerks and treasury officials when he was on military campaigns in Scotland. The way in which this upper floor was arranged can be seen either from the ground floor or from the wall walk (reached by the staircase near the entrance). The original floor level is indicated by the sills of the doorways and the paved ledges at the base of the wide window embrasures. Each lobe had two windows and a spiral staircase leading up to the wall walk. The north and west lobes also contain latrines. There is no evidence of fireplaces on this floor. The rooms may have been unheated, relying on braziers or portable hand-warmers, or they may have had fireplaces consisting of tiles set on a clay platform placed on the wooden floor, very like the cooking hearths found on some medieval ships.

Go up the spiral staircase to the wall walk if you have not already done so. The present wall-top is about 60cm (2ft) below its medieval level. This is the result of demolition work carried out in 1596 by the prison gaoler, Robert Redhead, who demolished parts of the castle and sold off its building materials, pocketing the payments himself. In order to conceal his

activities inside the tower he removed the internal partitions, the inner face and some wall core, but left the outside face intact. His activities were eventually stopped by the energetic protests of the mayor and corporation of York, but not before he had removed the turrets, battlements and roof, as well as some outworks to the south of the bailey.

Repairs to the wall-top can be identified by white stone, dating from the Civil War refurbishment, and a grey-brown gritstone reused by the Office of Works following the demolition of the nineteenth-century prison in 1935 (see page 24).

Wall Walk

Looking into the interior of the keep it is easy to appreciate how the upper floor was more spacious than the lower: the walls are thinner and the window recesses wider, thereby giving extra room to each lobe of the tower.

The wall walk also provides an excellent viewpoint from which to survey York and the surrounding countryside. From the centre of the east lobe (see plan, left), you look over the Walmgate suburb punctuated by the Victorian spire of St Lawrence's church. From the north lobe a panorama of the city is dominated by the Minster in the middle distance, with the open-work lantern of All Saints Pavement and the spire of St Mary Castlegate in the foreground. From the west lobe the red-brick Law Courts fill the foreground, while behind them runs the river Ouse with the warehouses, churches and houses of Micklegate and Bishophill on the further bank. Note the base of an arrow slit to the right of the information panel and the spout of a gargoyle to the left. Moving southwards, the tree-covered mound of Baile Hill can be seen across the river from Skeldergate bridge.

Looking out from the south lobe it is possible to appreciate the strategic position of this castle at the junction of two rivers. Today the wide flood plain of the Ouse stretches towards Selby and the cooling towers and chimneys of two power stations beside the Aire.

From the spectacular vantage point of the wall walk it is easy to understand why the sixteenth-century inhabitants of York objected so strongly to Redhead's plundering of the tower, which they described as 'a very rare mount, an exceeding ornament to the city'.

Chapel

A spiral staircase leads down from the wall walk to the chapel which is located over the entrance passage. There is no public access to this room but visitors may look in through the door. Only two of

the walls are original: they feature arcading consisting of four pointed arches with nail-head ornament. The altar would have been lit by the surviving window in the east wall (opposite), another window in the west wall (where you are standing) and two further windows in the south wall (to your right). There is a cupboard for

holy vessels in the north wall (to your left); the window opening above it allowed the occupants of the first floor to view the conduct of worship. In 1327 this chamber was replastered to provide accommodation for the queen mother, Isabella of France.

The position of the chapel above the entrance passage meant that the portcullis, when raised, would have been lifted directly

BELOW *An imaginary scene showing a service in progress in the chapel. Some of the original wall arcading survives (drawing: Peter Dunn)*

LEFT *The interior of the chapel today*

into it. The chapel could only have been used when the portcullis was down, and even so, the chains passing through the room would have been a serious hindrance to worship unless fully screened off. This might suggest that the use of the room as a chapel was an afterthought and that the arcading was transferred from an earlier chapel in the castle bailey in about 1300. (However, at Harlech and Caernarvon castles in Wales the portcullis is also raised through the chapel.) Originally the ceiling would have been much lower, with an upper room above; you can see the two narrow rectangular windows of this upper room in the south and west walls. The spiral staircase in the south-west corner of the tower was built in the seventeenth century.

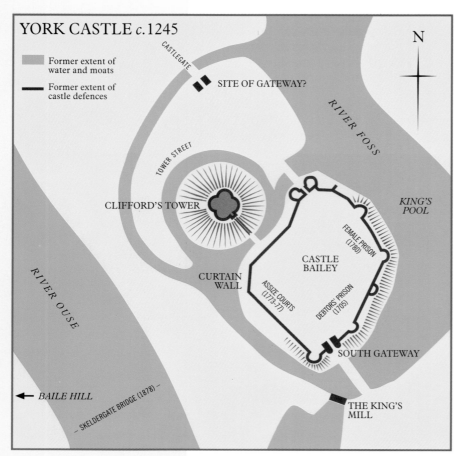

YORK CASTLE *c.* 1245

- Former extent of water and moats
- Former extent of castle defences

N

CASTLEGATE

SITE OF GATEWAY?

TOWER STREET

RIVER FOSS

CLIFFORD'S TOWER

KING'S POOL

RIVER OUSE

CURTAIN WALL

CASTLE BAILEY

FEMALE PRISON (1780)

ASSIZE COURTS (1773-77)

DEBTORS' PRISON (1705)

SOUTH GATEWAY

BAILE HILL

SKELDERGATE BRIDGE (1878)

THE KING'S MILL

ABOVE *The north turret with its latrine chute emptying outside the tower*

EXTERIOR

Outside the forebuilding, before descending the steep staircase down the mound, look at the buildings below you to get an impression of the layout of the medieval castle. Directly opposite the forebuilding three blocks of eighteenth-century buildings mark out the extent of the bailey or courtyard of York Castle. In the Middle Ages this area was protected by an earth bank with a timber stockade on top, enclosing free-standing buildings such as halls, kitchens, barns, stores and stables. During the thirteenth century the stockade was replaced by a stone curtain wall with six interval towers and two twin-towered gateways. Some of these still survive behind the Debtors' Prison and are described below. At the same period the wooden buildings were replaced in stone and positioned closer to the curtain wall.

When first constructed the castle was completely surrounded by water defences; the intrusion of modern roads and bridges makes it difficult to appreciate its initial isolation. To the left the river Foss still flows between the castle and the workshops and offices of Piccadilly. Originally the river was diverted into the King's Pool, a great artificial lake which fed water into the castle moats and acted as a fishpond (see plan, left). The Foss also drove the water mills to the south of the castle. Flood damage made necessary frequent repairs to the mill wheels, and they were eventually replaced by a steam engine in 1778.

The river Foss was made navigable shortly before 1800, allowing flour to be brought in from outside the city, and as a result the mills declined. The King's Pool was drained and built on, and the narrow Fossgate was replaced by the wider street of Piccadilly to link the city to the suburb of Walmgate. With the construction of a new bridge over the Foss at Castle Mills and the new Skeldergate bridge over the Ouse, the castle became surrounded by roads instead of moats.

Across the river Ouse you can see the tree-covered mound of the other Norman castle, Baile Hill, controlling the Skeldergate postern gate in the city walls.

The three neoclassical buildings in the courtyard are the Debtors' Prison of 1705, with its clock tower and cupola (opposite), the Assize Courts of 1773–77 (on the right) and the Female Prison of 1780 (on the left). This group of buildings, although much later in date than the medieval castle, emphasises the continuing status of the castle as a centre for law and order. The Assize Courts and Female Prison were designed by the celebrated York architect John Carr (1723–1807) who was responsible for many of the public buildings and town houses in the city. Both the Debtors' Prison and the Female Prison are today open to the public as museums maintained by York District Council. The Female Prison contains the interesting Kirk Collection of Bygones and a recreated Victorian street.

The design of Clifford's Tower itself can be appreciated by descending the mound and walking anti-clockwise round its base, through the car park and along the surrounding pavement of Tower Street. You can see the tower's fine stonework of magnesian limestone and the sloping plinth at its base. Each foil or lobe has two windows on the ground floor; originally these were tall thin arrow slits with circular openings at top and bottom, but later, in order to admit more daylight, the upper opening was made into a square window. The windows on the upper floor vary in size and must reflect the greater importance of the room nearest the entrance. At the junctions of the lobes are small rounded turrets or bartizans, supported on large stone corbels. These would

have continued above the wall walk with a battlemented storey, similar to the turrets on the main gates of the city. The two turrets nearer the entrance contain circular staircases lit by tall narrow windows. The north turret contains a latrine lit by a small square window and there are two latrines below it on the ground floor; their discharge chutes emptied just above the grass. High on the north-west lobe is the only surviving gargoyle, positioned to carry rainwater away from the wall-walk.

By walking a little further you can also see traces of the castle's outer defences. Near the present pedestrian crossing was the Castlegate postern, a gate in the city wall (see illustration on pages 20–21). The city wall forms the boundary of Tower Place and runs down to the square Davy Tower beside the river. Continuing along Tower Street towards the traffic roundabout, the back wall of the Assize Courts on the left follows the line of the castle

curtain wall; the grass bank was part of the outer defences, with a second, lower battlemented wall where the pavement now is and the wet moat near where Tower Street now runs. Beyond the Assize Courts is another small postern gate leading into these outer defences. You can also see the white limestone curtain wall, patched with bands of brown sandstone, together with a substantial corner tower standing nearly to its full height with some original arrow slits.

Beyond the tower and the garden railings is the basement of the twin-towered South Gateway, which led by a bridge across the moats to St George's Fields and the castle's corn mills. Another round tower with some original windows and arrow slits stands beyond this gate. Walling at the back of the Female Prison again incorporates the medieval curtain wall of white limestone. This now stands on the edge of a garden which can be approached through the Castle Museum.

ABOVE *Even today Clifford's Tower is an imposing building which dominates the surrounding area. The medieval tower, built in magnesian limestone, is seen here from the south*

9

THE VALE OF YORK was relatively unattractive to prehistoric settlers. Throughout the two millennia before the birth of Christ they preferred the drier soils of the chalk Wolds to the east or the limestone ridge to the west. The broad glacial trough that formed the Vale was characterised by bad drainage, poor soils and areas of heathland, open forest and swamps. A ridge of better gravel soils, the result of a glacial moraine, ran east to west across the Vale near Escrick. Some prehistoric settlement may have been established at York where the Ouse, swollen by its tributaries the Nidd and the Ure, had broken through this moraine. In 1902–3, during an operation to shore up the mound of Clifford's Tower, a skeleton was found buried in a crouched position in a coffin formed by sandstone slabs. Such burials are usually characteristic of the Bronze Age (2000–500 BC).

Roman York

The first phase of the Roman invasion of Britain was limited to southern and midland England, with the boundary drawn from the Humber estuary to the Bristol Channel and Exmouth. From AD 43–71 the conquest of the south was consolidated. But following revolts among the East Anglian Iceni tribe, supported by the Brigantes of northern England, the Romans decided to advance northwards. For this they used the Ninth Legion, transferring it from Lincoln to a new fortress, *Eboracum*, on the north bank of the Ouse. A major river crossing was established at Brough-on-Humber near the present Humber Bridge and a road network was developed throughout the Vale of York and across the Pennines to Manchester and Chester. The river system enabled supplies to be obtained from the Rhineland and Gaul.

The legionary fortress of *Eboracum* was built north-east of the river Ouse with the headquarters building just south of the site now occupied by York Minster. The present-day Petergate and Stonegate occupy the lines of the two main streets crossing the Roman fortress and Bootham Bar

stands on the site of the west gate. Built initially in earth and timber, the fortress was of a standard plan, rectangular with rounded corners and with watch towers at regular intervals. In the second century the walls were rebuilt in stone. These walls survive beneath the later, medieval walls on the west and north sides of the city. They can best be seen in the Museum Gardens and behind the public library. The Multangular Tower at the south-west corner of the fortress still stands up to 5m (17ft) in height and a stretch of the south wall of the fortress is also visible.

By the early third century the area to the south-west of the fortress on the opposite bank of the Ouse had been established as a *colonia*, initially a civilian settlement for retired soldiers and their families. The land to the east was used for burials, as were the fields on either side of the main approach roads. Decorated and inscribed stone coffins have been found on the site later occupied by York Castle, together with two wooden coffins and another of lead.

York gained in importance as the main base from which soldiers could be sent on campaign into Scotland or to gain rapid access to either end of the frontier along Hadrian's Wall. This importance was recognised in the fourth century when York became the capital of the province of *Valentia*, probably named in honour of the emperor Valentinianus. In 306 the emperor Constantius

ABOVE *The Multangular Tower, one of the corner towers of the Roman fortress of* Eboracum

YORK ARCHAEOLOGICAL TRUST

RIGHT *Coin dating from the reign of Constantius Chlorus, who died at York in AD 306*

BELOW RIGHT *An interval tower in the Roman fortress wall as it might have appeared when under construction in about AD 210 (drawing: Tracey Croft)*

BELOW *Plan of York showing settlement in the Roman, Anglian and Viking periods*

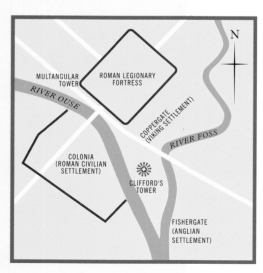

MULTANGULAR TOWER

RIVER OUSE

ROMAN LEGIONARY FORTRESS

N

COPPERGATE (VIKING SETTLEMENT)

RIVER FOSS

COLONIA (ROMAN CIVILIAN SETTLEMENT)

CLIFFORD'S TOWER

FISHERGATE (ANGLIAN SETTLEMENT)

Chlorus died at York and his son was proclaimed by the garrison. This son, Constantine, was to go on to found a new Rome in the east: Constantinople or Byzantium. His conversion to Christianity led to the establishment of bishoprics and cathedrals in all the major cities of the empire; this probably included York, which would have had a cathedral in or near the headquarters building.

The threat of barbarian invasions after 369 further enhanced the status of York. The *Dux Britanniorum* (a military leader) used the fort as a base from which to dispatch troops to any threatened part of the Yorkshire coast; advance warning would be given by a chain of signal stations established between the Tees and Flamborough Head.

Saxon York

Rome eventually succumbed to barbarian attacks, leaving the British to fend for themselves from the early fifth century. A few names of the post-Roman rulers of York are known. The conquest of the region by the Anglian King Edwin was followed by his acceptance of Christianity and baptism at *Eoforwic* (York) in 627. The church in which this took place probably stood just south of the present Minster, where a burial ground aligned on the Roman street plan has been found. Recent excavations in Fishergate on the east bank of the Foss have shown substantial evidence of an Anglian or Northumbrian trading settlement with wooden buildings and metalled streets. This settlement might have been the Roman *vicus*, or trading centre, that customarily stood outside a fortress, later adapted to become the Saxon *wic*; it may well have extended as far as the castle site.

Trade along the Ouse and Humber attracted another group of settlers. The Vikings raided the east coast from 797 and captured York in 866. They developed trade with Scandinavia and the Rhineland, and left their most enduring mark on the city in their name for it – *Jorvic*. They also named many of the streets or 'gates'. Plentiful evidence of Danish occupation has been found in the form of organic remains such as wood and leather preserved in damp soil: the houses in Coppergate and the wharves in Hungate yielded much information about daily

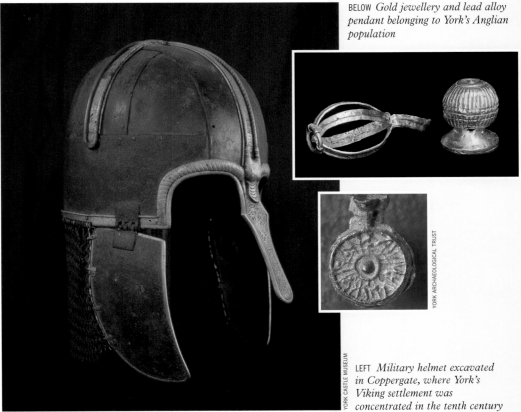

BELOW *Gold jewellery and lead alloy pendant belonging to York's Anglian population*

LEFT *Military helmet excavated in Coppergate, where York's Viking settlement was concentrated in the tenth century*

life and overseas trade during this period. The Jorvik Viking Centre (see inside back cover) is devoted to recreating the atmosphere of the time, displaying many of the artefacts found such as worked bone, glass, amber, silk and high-quality Rhineland pottery. An oxbone carved with Viking interlaced patterns was found on the site of the castle.

Although the city and region changed hands between Viking and Saxon groups six times between 952 and 1066 it remained a predominantly Viking area and was receptive to adventurers from Scandinavia and Viking Ireland. When Edward the Confessor died early in 1066 the throne of England was seized by Harold Godwineson of Wessex, but Harold's brother Tostig joined Harald Hardrada, King of Norway, in an invasion of the North which sailed up the Humber as far as Riccall. The Norse overcame the local defenders led by Earls Edwin and Morcar at the battle of Gate Fulford, 3km (2 miles) south of York. Harold Godwineson hurriedly marched his army north from London and defeated the invaders at Stamford Bridge on the river Derwent 12km (7 miles) east of York. But he was forced to return south immediately, to face the invasion of Duke William of Normandy.

THE NORMAN CASTLE

ABOVE *William the Conqueror, as portrayed in the Bayeux Tapestry. William built two castles at York and devastated the surrounding country in order to subdue his northern subjects*

ABOVE *The military campaigns of 1066 (in grey) and 1068–69 (in red)*

WILLIAM THE CONQUEROR'S victory at Hastings resulted in the establishment of Norman rule over wealthy southern England, but the outcome in Northumbria and Yorkshire was not a foregone conclusion. It needed two visits to York by William I and the devastation of the region, known as the 'Harrying of the North', before peace was established. This show of force was designed both to subdue the local population by impressing on them the superior military power of the Norman mounted warrior, and to deter any further Scandinavian claimants to the throne by destroying the local food supply. Even so it was a slow process to complete the conquest of the lands north of the river Tees.

William's campaign focused on York, which was the main city of the region, and second only to London in importance. Here he built the first royal castle in 1068, followed by a second in early 1069 to control the *colonia* (the settlement on the opposite bank of the Ouse), as well as the river approach to the main fortress.

In the autumn of 1069, however, a Danish fleet sailed up the Humber towards York, repeating the invasion of three years earlier. The local population, both within the city and in the neighbouring countryside, rose up in support and surrounded the castles. To deny shelter to the attackers the Norman garrisons set fire to nearby houses but the flames soon roared out of control. The garrisons were overwhelmed and the Danes, together with their local allies, dismantled the castles. The king immediately organised a relief expedition, but on his arrival outside the gates of the city found it deserted. It was then that William unleashed the revenge that came to be known as the 'Harrying of the North', laying waste to the entire region and sending out a stern message to future rebels.

Throughout his newly conquered kingdom the castle was the main means by which the king controlled the countryside and the major towns. In Yorkshire William was the biggest landowner, with estates scattered throughout the county, and castles in the largest city (York), the biggest port (Scarborough) and the best hunting ground (Pickering). His chain of castles dominated lines of communication by river and road. In his absence he appointed constables to administer his property; at York this was usually the sheriff of Yorkshire. Elsewhere in the county land was given to his warrior companions, the Norman barons, who built their own castles, founded new towns and established new monasteries in place of those destroyed by Viking raiders.

Some castles, built on rocky headlands, were constructed in stone from the outset, as at Richmond and Scarborough, but the majority

were built speedily using earth and timber, as happened at York. The normal pattern was the motte and bailey. The motte was an artificial mound of earth which supported a timber tower. The tower, of two or three storeys, held stores and weapons, with its topmost platform being used as a look-out and sentry post. This arrangement emphasised the king's dominion: it was the visible sign of lordship marked by his personal banner. The tower would often be surrounded by a fence or palisade with a wall walk allowing soldiers to fight from an advantageous position. The mound would be reached by a flight of wooden steps up its side or else by a 'flying bridge' spanning the moat from the bailey bank to the summit of the motte.

The bailey was a courtyard protected by a similar palisade and a defensive wall walk. Within it would be situated all the buildings necessary for defence, for the conduct of daily life on a royal or baronial scale, and for the administration of justice. These would include halls, kitchens, a chapel, barracks, stores, stables, forges, workshops and a prison, together with a reliable water supply. Outside would be a broad water-filled moat or a steep-sided dry ditch. The major castle at York must have satisfied all these requirements.

The city was also secured by new defences consisting of earthen banks erected above the earlier Roman walls and on the existing newer banks such as Aldwark. It is likely that the four gates or 'bars' of the city were built in stone at this period, possibly reusing Roman masonry. Many of the churches were rebuilt by the Normans after the fire of 1069. The three major

Norman buildings were the Minster, constructed by Archbishop Thomas of Bayeux, St Mary's Abbey, the foundations of which can be seen in the Museum Gardens, and Holy Trinity Priory in Micklegate where part of the early church is still visible. These buildings created a new skyline which dominated the city. Portions of stone-built merchants' houses also survive. Surprisingly, however, the castle keep and outer defences remained in timber until the thirteenth century.

The importance of the city increased throughout the twelfth century and soon York was pressing to manage its own affairs. Early in the reign of Henry II, between 1154 and 1158, the city obtained its first charter. This may have prompted the building of new defences which took place at about this time; the newly independent inhabitants would have been anxious to protect their prosperous city, and now had the tax-raising powers to do so. Henry II stayed in York at regular intervals, most frequently in pursuit of his war against the Scots. In 1175, for example, he came to York to receive the homage of William the Lion, King of the Scots – an important gesture of submission. Additionally the castle housed a mint to issue the silver pennies of the Norman kings. This was a continuation of the practice of the Saxon rulers dating from the reign of Athelstan (925–941) and of the Viking kings of York.

As a royal stronghold the castle came under royal jurisdiction, and was subject neither to the administrative authority of the city nor to that of one of the three Ridings of Yorkshire, whose boundaries converged on the city.

ABOVE *The city of York's first charter, issued by Henry II in the 1150s*

LEFT *A reconstruction drawing showing the possible appearance of the timber tower and bailey, as built in the late eleventh century on the orders of William the Conqueror (drawing: Terry Ball)*

13

THE JEWS OF YORK

ABOVE *The Jews under attack in this medieval manuscript illustration are identified by the distinctive badges on their clothes*

ABOVE *This house in Lincoln is traditionally described as having belonged to Aaron the Jew. Its strong stone walls would have been necessary for security. The houses of York's leading Jews, such as Josce the financier, may well have been similar in appearance*

BELOW *Manuscript illustration of Norwich Jews dating from 1233. The caricatures display the antisemitism which reached a peak during the reigns of the crusader kings Richard I and Edward I*

THE TIMBER TOWER of York Castle, the precursor of Clifford's Tower, witnessed the most horrible event in the history of English Jewry. In March 1190 the city's entire Jewish community took shelter in the castle and, when threatened by a violent mob outside, many took their own lives. Those who surrendered were murdered.

The first Jews had come to England in the wake of the Norman Conquest and settled in London. With the encouragement and protection of Henry II Jewish business activity had flourished, especially money-lending. The numbers of settlers gradually increased and the Jews spread out into the provinces, with bases in the main cities of Norwich, Lincoln and York. Indeed York may have been a 'branch outlet' of Aaron of Lincoln's money-lending business.

There were two main reasons for the establishment of a Jewish community in York. The first was the existence of an important royal castle, which could offer the king's protection in times of persecution. The second was the emergence amongst the barons, gentry and monasteries in Yorkshire of the need for financial credit. Christians were forbidden from engaging in money-lending or usury. The Jews filled this economic role.

From the mid-1170s Jews were buying property in York. Their leader was Josce of York, a financier whose house 'rivalled a noble citadel in the scale and stoutness of construction'. Another usurer and bond-dealer was Benedict, while religious scholarship was encouraged by Rabbi Yomtob from Joigny in France. These three men were prominent in a community of some thirty households of approximately 150 people. However, life for the Jewish groups in England was punctuated by outbreaks of religious attacks, usually

prompted by false accusations of ritual murder. The death of their protector Henry II in 1189 and the coronation of the crusader king, Richard I, led to propaganda not only against the external Moslem 'pagan' but against the internal Jewish 'infidel'. An anti-Jewish riot broke out on the coronation day and the London Jewish quarter was set alight with the loss of at least thirty lives. Benedict of York had been injured in the riot and died at Northampton on his journey home. The London riot was followed by others in King's Lynn and Norwich in February 1190. York repeated the same pattern early in March.

The events began on a stormy night when a band of armed men broke into the house of the recently deceased Benedict of York. They killed his widow and children, carried off his treasure and set the roof alight. Fearing for their lives the York Jews, led by Josce, sought royal protection within York Castle. Several days later, as the rioting and plunder continued, the terrified Jews refused entry to the constable of the castle, fearing he would hand them over to the sheriff with his armed retainers, or to the frenzied mob. After a gallant defence of ten or more days they saw siege engines being brought into position and knew their position was hopeless. On the night of Friday 16 March, the eve of the Jewish 'great Sabbath' before Passover, Rabbi Yomtob called upon his fellow Jews to commit suicide rather than suffer their inevitable murder. The majority of the Jews followed his advice, in an action reminiscent of the suicide of the Jews on Mount Masada in Israel in AD 74.

This mass suicide was accompanied by a raging fire intended to destroy the tower of the castle and to cremate the Jews' bodies so that they could not be dismembered. A few survivors surrendered on the promise of Christian baptism but they were massacred by a gang of 'cruel butchers'. The horror of this attack was recorded by many chroniclers, notably the monk William of Newburgh whose

monastery stood between Helmsley and York.

Although the king punished the sheriff of Yorkshire, John Marshall, and the constable of the castle by dismissing them from their posts, the real ring-leader was a man named Richard Malebisse, and his fellow conspirators were Yorkshire gentry and important landlords. They made use of the popular antisemitism as a screen to cancel out their debts to the Jews. They were also protesting about royal protection of the 'infidels' at a time when they themselves had been denied such royal privileges. It seems that the conspirators were never brought to justice though the city was fined heavily for its part in the massacre.

Despite this episode Jews were willing to return and live in the city, because they identified business opportunities among the barons, the gentry and the expanding religious houses. Cistercian abbeys such as Rievaulx relied heavily on the credit advanced by the Jews of York. The community grew until another crusading king, Edward I, introduced the Statute of Jewry in 1275, which made the practice of usury illegal and thus effectively put the Jews out of business. A survey made in that year suggests that the Jewish population was then about 150 – the same as at the time of the 1190 massacre. In 1290, however, Edward I ordered that 'all the Jews of our kingdom' leave the country in 'perpetual exile'. By then only six property-holders remained in York. Their assets were seized and sold; ironically the proceeds from the sales of Jewish property throughout England were used in part to glaze new windows at Westminster Abbey.

A final insight into the medieval Jewish community in York was provided by the recent excavation of their cemetery at Jewbury. The remains of nearly 500 skeletons were recorded and analysed, revealing that anaemia and tuberculosis were common in the community. Their bones were subsequently reinterred in a plot at the edge of the original cemetery.

On the night of Friday 16 March 1190 some
150 Jews and Jewesses of York having sought
protection in the Royal Castle on this site
from a mob incited by Richard Malebisse
and others chose to die at each other's
hands rather than renounce their faith
שימו לך כבוד ותהלתו באיים
ISAIAH XLII 12

THE BUILDING OF CLIFFORD'S TOWER

ABOVE *The castle of Etampes lies 48km (30 miles) south of Paris. The design was copied at Clifford's Tower*

After the fire

The burning of the wooden tower in 1190 left York Castle without its strongpoint. Richard I immediately ordered the damage to be repaired and between 1190 and 1194 more than £200 was spent on the castle. The 'King's Tower' was rebuilt in timber and the summit of the motte was raised by 4m (13ft) using a dense layer of clay.

King John stayed in the castle in 1200 and again later in his reign when he sought shelter from civil unrest. The recent repairs were evidently not entirely satisfactory because in 1228 there is a record of the castle gate being in ruin and the tower on the motte flattened by high winds.

The new stone castle

After a visit in 1244, prompted by the threat of war with the Scots, Henry III decided to rebuild the entire castle in stone. He ordered his master mason Henry de Rayns and his chief carpenter Simon of Northampton, who were then working on Windsor Castle, to inspect the castle in March 1245 and arrange for rebuilding to be undertaken. The sheriff of Yorkshire, who was responsible for all the necessary payments, was to consult these and other experts to ensure that the castle was strengthened according to their advice. In the course of the following twenty years over £2450 was spent on the construction of Clifford's Tower, the bailey walls, seven towers, two gates and their bridges, two halls, a kitchen, a chapel and a prison. Some earlier work in stone had been carried out between 1200 and 1204; this may have been on the north gate and its approach bridge towards Castlegate. Later, between 1237 and 1241, a prison for women with a chapel over it was built in the bailey; it is probable that this was also in stone.

Henry de Rayns chose a four-leaved design for Clifford's Tower. This was derived directly from the French castle of Etampes. The two-storeyed tower, with its four leaves (or lobes), its three rounded turrets and its battlements, would have made an impressive outline against the sky, emphasising royal power across the city. The tower was enclosed by a wooden palisade (or fence) topped by a wall walk, and was linked to the outer bailey by a wooden stair and a bridge over the moat.

The first mention of the new structure in the royal accounts was in 1251 when the sheriff was ordered to allocate 300 marks (£200) to work on

ABOVE *The keep of Pontefract Castle in West Yorkshire is a larger and more ornate version of the four-leaved design and was built after Clifford's Tower. This painting dates from 1630*

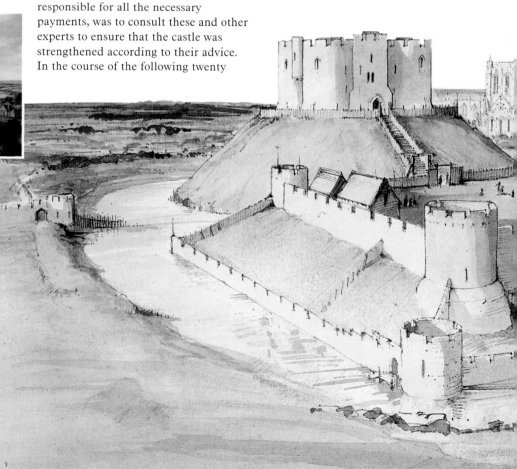

the castle, including work on the 'Great Tower'. Timber for floor or roof joists was required in 1259 and more timber was needed in 1269–72, by which time the tower was substantially complete. In 1312 the chapel within the tower needed new roof lead; this may have been when the wall arcading seen in the chapel today was transferred from an earlier chapel in the bailey (see page 7). The palisade and outer ditch around the castle were completed in that same year. However, the tower was already in use in 1298 during Edward I's campaigns against the Scots, as a stronghold for the king's treasury (that is, the money raised through taxes and the officers responsible for it). The tower was used for the same purpose in 1322 under Edward II and in 1361–2 under Edward III.

Soon after Edward II's defeat at Bannockburn in 1314 his castle in York was seriously undermined. Severe floods in 1315–16 had softened the soil at the base of the artificial motte, making urgent repairs necessary. The same problem was reported in January 1360 when the castle was 'cracked from top to bottom in two places'. These cracks, which are still visible on the south lobe, were attributed to the decay of the foundations. The royal surveyors recommended that the tower be pulled down and rebuilt as new, but instead it was repaired over the next five years at a cost of £200. The problems did not end there, however: there are regular mentions throughout the fourteenth century of further repairs to the leadwork on the roofs and to the woodwork of the palisades,

bridge and hoardings within the tower. Ironwork on the doors, locks and windows also needed regular expenditure. The most unusual repair was the order in 1327 for plastering a room over the entrance to the castle as a residence for the queen mother, Isabella of France. This must refer to the former chapel, which would have provided secure accommodation preventing its occupant from escape. (Although Isabella was acting as regent for her son, Edward III, at this time, he did not trust her and wanted to control her movements.)

The frequent reference to this tower as the 'King's Tower' stresses that it was exclusively for royal use, unlike the bailey which was used by the sheriff or constable to administer justice throughout the county. When the tower was still in good repair the king would have stayed here, but from the time of Edward I onwards kings more often stayed in the Franciscan friary in Castlegate, while the royal officials lodged in other monasteries – St Mary's Abbey just west of the city and St Andrew's Priory in Fishergate.

The clearest indication that the tower was the place in which the king's justice was dispensed was the decision to make this the site for the display of the body of the political rebel Roger de Clifford. Clifford was hanged in chains from the summit of the tower in 1322. In July 1537 the body of Robert Aske, who had led the religious rebellion known as the Pilgrimage of Grace, was similarly exposed. By this time the King's Tower was 'all in ruine' and quite unsuitable for living in.

ABOVE *King Henry III confers with his architects. Henry was largely responsible for the rebuilding of York Castle in stone*

LEFT *The stone castle as it may have appeared on its completion in the early fourteenth century. Compare this with the timber version on pages 12–13 (drawing: Terry Ball)*

CASTLE BUILDING IN THE LATER MIDDLE AGES

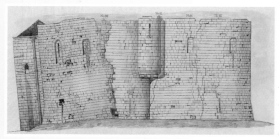

ABOVE *The east elevation of Clifford's Tower, drawn in 1913. The cracking and tilting of the south lobe, caused by subsidence, was first reported in 1315*

THE PROCESS of building the stone castle was a considerable undertaking and involved assembling numerous workmen with a wide variety of skills. For example, except where rivers were being used as natural defences, the ditches around the bailey and keep needed to be specially dug. For this task skilled ditch-diggers from the fenland districts of Lincolnshire and Cambridgeshire were summoned, together with men from the marshlands of Holderness in east Yorkshire. Carpenters were brought in to make defensive palisades, floors, roofs and scaffolding. They first trimmed the timbers with axes, then cut the planks in the saw-pit and smoothed them with planes. The timber frames were secured with wooden pegs, the peg-holes being made with an auger (a tool for boring).

In emergencies, such as the threat of war, doors, window shutters, bridges and projecting wooden galleries (or 'brattices') could often be brought to the castle prefabricated.

For the stonework, the master mason first had to choose his material at one of the 'York stone' quarries on the limestone ridge west of Tadcaster. The quarried stone was then brought by cart or more usually by barge along the rivers Wharfe and Ouse directly to the castle. After labourers had unloaded the stone, the masons trimmed the ashlars (the carefully hewn blocks used as cornerstones and in other places where a smooth finish was required). The finer details of door and window openings, arrow slits, corbels and battlements would have been finished at the masons' bench in a shed inside the bailey. Workmen would then have hoisted or dragged the stones on to the scaffold wherever they were needed and the stone-layers would have mortared the ashlars into their correct place. Larger arches would have been supported on a timber framework. The masons' lads would have been kept busy mixing the mortar and keeping it moist. The ingredients for the mortar would have been prepared on site; many castles still have the lime kilns used to burn the limestone into powder.

Two other specialised crafts were those of the blacksmiths and the plumbers. The smiths were responsible for making all the nails, bolts, staples, door-hinges, window-bars and hinge-pins needed on site. Some items, such as the vast quantities of nails and the special door locks, would have been made close to the source of iron in the forest forges. Over 43,000 nails of twelve different types were bought for York Castle in 1327. The smiths had the additional tasks of sharpening all the workmen's tools, grinding the chisels down to provide a sharp blade and mending cracked axe-heads.

Plumbers were required to install lead sheets on the roofs, spouts to carry rainwater away from the wall tops and

LEFT *Building work in progress in the castle bailey, as it may have appeared in the late thirteenth century. The mason's shed in the foreground is being used to prepare the stone blocks and hoists on the towers lift them into position (drawing: Peter Dunn)*

on St George's Day 1684, when the cannon on the roof were fired in celebratory salute. That same night all the woodwork of the tower caught fire and some of the gunpowder stored inside it exploded. Some suspected that this was an act of deliberate arson by the local townsfolk, who had become hostile to the military presence in their city and were no longer proud of the medieval tower, derisively calling it 'the minced pie'. The resulting damage was so serious that the tower could no longer accommodate a royal garrison.

The presence of the garrison had in any case been in question since 1682, when a report by Sir Christopher Musgrave, Lieutenant General of Ordnance, had recommended its withdrawal since it would cost over £30,000 to bring the medieval castle up to modern artillery standards. The surveyor's plan accompanying this report shows a proposal for six angled bastions arranged regularly around the bailey walls, but there is no evidence that any of these was built. The report recommended that Clifford's Tower itself be retained, because of its commanding position over the city, and suggested that it 'might be made very defensible for a small charge'. Nothing was done, however. The tower continued to be staffed by a token garrison until peace was restored following the landing of William III (the Dutch ruler William of Orange) in 1688. Clifford's Tower then passed into private hands.

From 1684 onwards the term York Castle was taken to refer only to the court and prison buildings in the bailey. The moat around Clifford's Tower – now dry – was gradually incorporated into the gardens of the houses in Castlegate, and soon after 1727 a local gentleman, Mr Samuel Waud, built an elegant four-storey town house at the junction of Castlegate and the present Tower Street. The motte and its tower became Romantic garden features of this new property; visitors could climb a winding shrub-lined path up the mound to the medieval tower, now wreathed in ivy (see illustration, page 22).

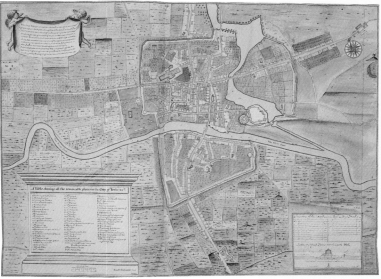

BELOW *A plan of York Castle by the surveyor Jacob Richards showing the six bastions proposed in 1682 but never built*

RIGHT *The neoclassical Assize Courts were built by the Yorkshire architect John Carr on the site of the old Grand Jury House*

BELOW *The Female Prison, also designed by Carr, now houses the Castle Museum*

ABOVE RIGHT *The Debtors' Prison was the first of the imposing new buildings constructed in the castle bailey area in the eighteenth century. It drew mixed comments from contemporary prison reformers*

RIGHT *By contrast with the bailey area, Clifford's Tower and its mound were reduced to garden features when they were incorporated into the property of Mr Samuel Waud, whose new house can be seen to the bottom right of this print of 1730*

THE EIGHTEENTH CENTURY saw major changes in the appearance of the administrative buildings in the bailey. The contrast between old and new was pronounced. While Clifford's Tower fell further into ruin, the courts and prisons were steadily improved. As York with its Assembly Rooms and elegant Mansion House became the natural centre for the social life of the county, so the castle area began to reflect this wealth and

status. At the start of the century both castle gateways were still standing and the four main buildings were the Grand Jury House, the Common Hall, the Chapel and the Prison. The first to be replaced was the prison: a new County Gaol was built between 1701 and 1705, probably to the designs of William Wakefield and of similar appearance to Vanbrugh's Royal Hospital at Greenwich. This building, which later became the Debtors' Prison, dwarfed the

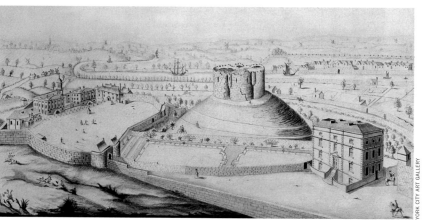